going out & being normal

going out &
being normal

poems by

Vaughn M. Watson

Press 53
Winston-Salem

Press 53, LLC
PO Box 30314
Winston-Salem, NC 27130

First Edition

A Tom Lombardo Poetry Selection

Going Out and Being Normal: Poems
Runner-Up for the 2025 Press 53 Award for Poetry

Cover art, "New York Sidewalk," by Lerone Pieters
Acquired for donation through Pexels

Author photograph by Kendra Irene
www.kendrairene.com

Library of Congress Control Number
2025932183

ISBN 978-1-950413-94-2

Contents

Preface   xi

I.
incident reports

first, love   3
border control   4
tourist trap   5
culture shock   6
fencing with Kierkegaard   8
no laughing matter   9
Orpheus and Eurydice   10
left behind   11

II.
poems of, for, and about

Poem of forgiveness for a family member who wronged you   15
Poem about being Black (for the market)   16
Poem about being Black (for myself)   17
Poem of China   18
中国之诗   19
Poem of surnames and their transliterations   20
Poem for queers   21
Poem for COVID dogs   22
Poem for airports   23
Poem for former grindr users   24
Poem of acceptance   25

III.
going out and being normal

sutras for the modern New Yorker   29
sad, sad story   30
if I loved you (68°F / 20°C)   31

fear of falling   32
snow day   33
the new Penn Station!   34
mother in her skin   35
man with a mission   36
out for a walk   37
W 4th Street   38

IV.
notes on

notes on narcissism   41
notes on composition   42
notes on disgust   43
notes on a walking commute   44
notes on attraction   45
notes on avoidant attachment   46
notes on carrying a bouquet of flowers on the D train   47
notes on intimacy   48
notes on aphantasia   49

V.
ars poetica

soft drink   53
*Soir Bleu*_Edward Hopper_(1914)   54
*Joan of Arc*_Jules Bastien-Lepage_(1879)   55
*Atlas*_Lee Lawrie_(1937)   56
*Untitled (Slide)*_Carsten Holler_(2011)   57
*Self-portrait*_Robert Pattinson_(2020)   58

Acknowledgments   61
Author Biography   63

Preface

this collection was born of my own anxiety. we emerged from COVID a society irrevocably changed. being alone, to an extrovert, is a type of trauma. etiquette seems to have faded away. the isolation of lockdowns became the isolation of an allegedly reintegrated world of commuters. and AirPods. people scrolling through TikTok as they walk their dogs. we're all doing our best, I think. to reintegrate, to reconcile with an unaddressed collective trauma. we're all going out and being normal. we're doing the best that we can.

I.

incident reports

first, love

His face was blank, a desktop monitor left untouched. Lips pink and pursed. More handsome behind a screen than in person. Maybe I fucked up. *You're really fucked up*, he said, opening Google Translate to find the word for "pick-up artist." I sat there and took it; it was what I deserved. I told him who I was, but he didn't listen. Twinks on PreP can do anything.

border control

You rifled through that tiny pocket within the front pocket of your jeans, then pulled out a tiny pouch of coke. Told me how you'd just flown from Thailand with it; that you'd forgotten about it, that the key was to just forget.

That one night in Kunming. We lived like kings. Checked our noses for white. Then emerged from the bathroom stall the life of the party. We conquered the dance floor. Cigarette after cigarette. All thanks to *you*. Every time I fill. The gray plastic bin. At the TSA checkpoint. I check my pockets. And check them well.

tourist trap

If you saw me amongst the French and Cariocas along 5th Avenue
all in search of holiday deals. String lights and shuttered offices. In a
glance, days spent: lost time waiting for trains to arrive.

If I plucked you from the crowd. We'd have clasped gloved hands.
Told each other things we haven't even told our partners. We'd know
we'd never see each other again, and we'd pretend this wasn't true.

culture shock

In Pedra do Sal, where the slaves used to party, piss and spilt caipirinhas make the stone steps glisten. I watch my friend Fabio lock eyes with a handsome Brazilian, a brown bear with glasses, then press up against him without exchanging a word. His hand cradled that brown bear's bald head as they kissed with a passion I'd only heard in song. And just as quickly, they pulled away. Took a sip of their Rum & Cokes. Just like nothing ever happened.

It is an indescribable moment, the instant of the feint. The opponent feels, as it were, the cut, he is struck; and so he is, but in a place quite different from what he thought.

—Søren Kierkegaard, *The Seducer's Diary*

fencing with Kierkegaard

Over happy hour drinks, I dismantle the awkwardness between us like a fencer removing her saturated gear. Disarm you with petty work gossip and talk of what's new. Thirty minutes and two well drinks later, the formality between us stands eroded.

I tell you with a glint in my eye just how handsome, how deserving of love you are. Then relish in how you fluster from this sudden lunge forward; the rubber-like bend of a foil—contact! You: hit where least anticipated. The buzzer buzzing. The round won.

no laughing matter

The northbound conductor confirms a southbound train has, indeed, smashed a deer to pieces. The passengers burst into laughter—from shock or, possibly, relief? I'm laughing too, though I don't know why. At the irony, maybe, of an express train to London eviscerating a deer on New Year's Day?

Orpheus and Eurydice

so close I could almost taste
the ashes in the air give
way to house dust—a future of
baseboards that just won't stay clean

I would have watched you
play your lyre through the kitchen
window—our love a texture
trickling steadily through a sieve

failure so close
to the underworld gates
is a sort of kindness, I guess

as great love, you once
sang, should vanish,
not fizzle out like
a pan of
rapeseed oil
atop a greasy stove

left behind

Imagine please the night sky
fill up with Rapturous light,

as I did for a few sleepless
weeks in my teens.

Herald of a whirling cloud,
UFO Messiah, abductor of societies.

With our luck, we'd be left
behind to wander:

faith undeserving
of salvation.

Believers traverse
illuminated skies;

we alone witness broken
seals and feral horsemen.

II.

poems of, for, and about

Poem of forgiveness for a family member who wronged you

You told me you wished I'd never been born. I carry it with me (i carry it in my heart). Family is tricky. On a good day, we sit, silent, as Jeopardy melds into Wheel of Fortune. On a shitty day, I am wished out of existence by someone on whose mine depends. Family be like: put some strangers in a 2 ½ bedroom co-op; try to make it work. That's your father, your cousin, your grandmother. Blood a scapegoat for words thrust as violently, as accurately as foils.

Poem about being Black (for the market)

Something about Emmett Till. This soaring chord of a gospel choir refuses to resolve. *And Still I Rise.* My grandmother tells me once again of the early '40s, when she was made to eat her ice cream on the stoop like a dog. Black Lives Matter. In June of 2023, Students for Fair Admission, Inc. successfully sued Harvard University to end affirmative action. And in Florida, it's time to move on and stop tarnishing the lily-white history of a nation.

In state after state, statue after statute will be removed. A bronze-plated Theodore Roosevelt accompanied by a Native American and a Sub-Saharan African was taken from the front steps of the American Museum of Natural History because "its composition suggested a racial hierarchy." *How To Be An Anti-Racist*: dismantle a statue. leave a commemorative plaque in its place. Atop a pristine patch of concrete.

Poem about being Black (for myself)

Being a person of color

is a series of moments

in America we

have to consider

each hurdle

might be the result

of generations

comprised of

very bad days

or maybe

it's just

as simple

as wrong place

wrong time

Poem of China

我第一次去中国的第一夜，
不知道能吃什么

机场里，我以为我很聪明，
到了城里才发现我竟然很笨

我真的什么都不知道，
我应该谦虚一点儿啊

五道口的十字路口人山人海，
各种味道，各种认不出的汉字

路上的带白帽的工人对我好冷漠呀
认不出的汉字，认不出的神情

让我越来越避之不及
天黑的时候什么都看不明白。

中国之诗

my first night in Beijing
all I wanted was something to eat

but neon characters suspended
in air stopped me dead in my tracks.

there are so many words I don't recognize
and so many faces I've never seen.

in the blackest night, you can't make out anything
—and that's what shatters your confidence.

Poem of surnames and their transliterations

阮 马 陈 李

姜 贺 刘 秦

黄 孙 陈 帝

扭 王 柴 魏

ruan ma yuan li
jiang he liu qin
huang sun chen di
niu wang chai wei

Poem for queers

leaning against bars, grabbing the same old well drink. sneakers unsticking from the unmopped floor. looking away, looking at looking away. quiet hugs in sketchy corners. a cheap leather harness protruding from beneath a t-shirt. getting weird looks. giving weird looks. open-mouth kisses on a makeshift dance floor. that grainy taste of alcohol on the breath. touching, being touched. in places you'd never imagined. only dreamed of and, upon waking, forced yourself to forget.

Poem for COVID dogs

to the shelter puppies, adopted by well-meaning mothers. to the doggie Xanax that keeps them both sane. to dogs that trot along on three legs, undeterred. to dogs that struggle to keep up with daddy's run. to dogs in strollers that I mistake for babies. dogs in kennels, dogs in crates. dogs that drool onto my sneakers on the subway. to dogs I've never held before, and never will. to dogs that nibble on tiny treats then sit and wait patiently for another.

Poem for airports

a TSA
check
point
serves as
survey of
America,

every
thing
wrong
with
her
people

Poem for former grindr users

smack-
dab
with-
in
end-
less
squares of
men

track
the prog-
ression
of his
user-
name
over
a day,
a week,
the years
& trace
his descent
into mad-
ness

Poem of acceptance

(*you*)th's pleasures, as Plath's *Bell Jar* figs, wither and fall to the ground[ing]:

the incremental realization that aging is a compulsory kind of self-care. that what you've got to do is embrace the *you* who always was. find solace in the crookedness of the body—how its limitations multiply.

lamentation for the *you* who believed a midnight trip to the Brookline 7-11 could be some sort of adventure. *you* who believed each night ought to be carried out fully, without regard for any emails lying ahead.

a *you* who is never coming back and a
you who has to be fine with that.

[a poem is a lie
that reveals
some universal
truth]

III.

going out and being normal

sutras for the modern New Yorker

My phone accidentally defined *be*
I read the sixteen definitions closely.

A life is the shape of a day;
the night is bitter and vicarious.

How to make dinner;
How to remove hard water stains.

This washing machine has run for
the longest four minutes of my life.

145 can look so
much like 149.

Countdown clocks;
digital route maps.

A tourist who almost sits in your lap on the train
is a tourist who orders a Venti ice water.

The line to the Times Square Margaritaville
wraps around the fucking corner.

The McDonald's bags we hold to our chests
are precious as newborn babes.

A Gen Z kind of youthful glow is earned,
not applied in spritzes.

Before a poster of a purple-red sphere
balancing amethyst in my palm.

Mind, I beg you:
comply with body.

Be more resilient than the branches of a mid-March tree;
resist winter's dying breath from this standing desk.

sad, sad story

unfortunately flight delayed

he texts his girlfriend
from the Terminal 5 Starbucks line
this sad, sad story
that I am somehow now a part of

they'll have to be apart
for a few more hours
at least he'll have his iced coffee
and I, my ham & cheese croissant

if I loved you (68°F / 20°C)

In the constant babbling of recycled Jersey spa water, the *how I loved you* in the final measures of Rodgers and Hammerstein's "If I Loved You." Everything below my neck submerged in those final lines—*how I loved you / if I loved you*. I cling to the ladder and once more try to enjoy the chill of frigid water.

Rush of the waterfall faucet that fills the temptress of a neighboring pool (100°F/37°C). After two minutes in the cold plunge, I'm told, what is wintry might feel warm and inviting. / *never, never to know*. To plunge into cold depths is to be victim of caprice. Shallow breaths, forceful gripping of the ladder: / *how I loved you*. Violent dunking of the neck, head, hair in one committed motion. Rupture of the water's surface / *if I loved you*. Hesitant body succumbs to unyielding mind.

fear of falling

for Jared Harél

Figure skaters dance to "The Dance of the Sugar Plum Fairy,"
their inertia maintained by slight wiggles at the hip.

I cling to the edges: stiff legs gripped by a fear of falling,
failing to let myself glide, to skate as if dancing.

Skating requires a kind of innocence like children
falling in heaps just to lie there out on the ice.

Or audacity like hockey team teenagers screeching
to a halt.

I want a return to the me I used to be,
to sail; to keep time knowing.

snow day

two paths lay before me:

one trodden by boots
blackened and wet

the other pristine;
paved with fresh, fresh snow!

I will be the first
to trod the powdery white

my filthy bootprint
the still-life of a commuter

the new Penn Station!

the relative coolness of this underground passage. 8th, 7th, 33rd.
an exit somewhere at the center of the labyrinth. of mismanaged
construction. I only catch glimpses of the familiar amidst constant
change. getting off the A, a crossroads.   the in-between space.
33rd between 8th, 7th. left, right, underground. trying to remember
which way I went last time. so I don't go that way. the joy of
discovering 6 ½ Avenue one hot summer day. to the left: fluorescent,
sterile—the new Penn Station, Moynihan Hall. to the right: decay of
subway brick I've always loved.

mother in her skin

this dyke on the train has a tattoo that reads: *Hey honey,*
it's Mom. I love you. See you soon in a cursive like a permission
slip's signature, emblazoned on the ashen skin of her inner forearm.
she reads it every now and then, in her mother's voice. I read it every
now and then, in my mother's voice. you read it every now and then,
in your mother's voice. live on, live on! the mother in her skin.

man with a mission

for Elvin

didn't I tell you

a friend of mine brought me

to see Man with a Mission,

the Japanese band?

that each skinny member   [

wore dark jeans, sneakers,   you

and the oversized head   my love,

of a furry, gray wolf?   a Japanese audience:
                                             silent and eager for

at the end of the concert,   the penultimate chord

they took to the mic;

told us how much louder   the bow, the *arigatou*

we were than crowds back home.   the neat resolution;

                                             hum of bass resounding

but we couldn't tell   off a too-still crowd

if they were egging us on

or trying to ask us to   ]

keep it down   lol

out for a walk

on the sloping street
high above Jackie Robinson Park,
a man cradles
a Dunkin' Donuts bag

further up Edgecombe
Yankee Stadium's all lit-up and navy blue:
big-box shops dot the Bronx;
the Frost Moon: a sky absent of stars.

above me, the last leaf of winter is
felled by an assertive breeze

below, I've trampled
a mound of dog shit

W 4th Street

for LZ

at 10:44 p.m. on a Thursday
I feel invincible

weaving through crowds
sucking a green apple vape

looking forward
to another wfh Friday

wondering if I am,
in fact, having a breakdown

what that
would even feel like

though I just witnessed
one last week irl

with my
own eyes

someone who simply
stopped making sense

who couldn't hear my words
over his inner voices

that alternated between
telling him

that he could do anything
that he could do nothing

can you
hear me

you can do anything
you can do anything

all you need to do is leave
this station and catch your bated breath

IV.

notes on

notes on narcissism

self
as seen by
self

reminds me:

how
self
sees
self

is
not
how
they
see
self

notes on composition

that shadow of a nimbus cloud

                    on that hill like a painting.
                    nature mimics art.
                    makes us
                    engage in
                    aesthetic attention.

that cloud,   that shadow,
                    that hill.

seen through my eyes.

worthy of a photograph or,
more fittingly,   a poem.

notes on disgust

at first I thought it might be some sort of fucked up leaf, or lost
beanie or torn-out weave. but on closer inspection, it's the corpse
of a rat. trampled by an e-bike or Uber or skateboard. I cannot
turn away from my disgust; I carry it with me into this poem. I sit
in front of a MacBook, try to figure out what it means to me. what
metaphor, what profundity might be found
in the disfigured corpse of a rat?

notes on a walking commute

- a park path can function as a homeless shelter;
  even in crisis, humans maintain order

- a pair of seagulls stalks the 1 train
  as it thunders out of a man-made cavern—
  round in circles they go

- a throng of business students armed with
  expensive umbrellas and a sense of
  entitlement that won't be dampened by rain

- a fog rolls in and swallows up
  Riverside Drive sometimes

- the color of the sky like the goo
  Westworld robots are made of

notes on attraction

for the really hot guy who never texted me

the breadth of your shoulders. how it accentuates the narrowness
of your belted waist. a sliver of tribal tattoo peeks through the
generous opening of
your dress shirt. I already miss the presence of your palm, that
seconds ago gripped
my shoulder. the way you lean against the bar the way I lean
against the bar

so that we are almost touching

notes on avoidant attachment

maybe I'm some kind of monster. born of childhood trauma. failed
therapy sessions of Chutes & Ladders. 100-piece puzzles with 99
pieces. all they really taught me is:
games have rules that shouldn't be broken.

notes on carrying a bouquet of flowers on the D train

for Makila Kirchner

even *I* start to wonder where I'm going

bearing a thoughtful
gift or cliché apology

I bring the soft,wet buds
to my face—smell them deeply

Would you hold me
where cheap plastic wrap
& rubber bands meet
neatly trimmed stems?

All the way across
Manhattan Bridge?

notes on intimacy

we roamed the Esplanade smoking poorly rolled joints. I brought
you back to my dorm without knowing what that meant. my
roommate was out. we talked beneath the Pulp Fiction poster. over
the unmade twin XL bed.

and when the talk ran out we sat there, not saying anything. you
looked away. I looked away. we were waiting for something, for
anything to happen.

notes on aphantasia

I tried to imagine a beach. its salty air, its grainy sand. the sound of
waves. nothing. in my mind. blinking cursor of a word processor.
text appearing without appearing. this memory: a block
of vanishing text. the smell of the sea contains a childhood
of unwritten phrases.

[i like
when you are serious and i
don't know
what you're thinking
about]

V.

ars poetica

soft drink

after William Carlos Williams

So much depends
upon

Pocari Sweat
an

energy drink
in

a blue and white
can

*Soir Bleu*_Edward Hopper_(1914)

sometimes I'm a clown
sometimes I'm a prostitute
either way, people keep staring

beneath Chinese lanterns
ashing a cigarette
I look into the distance
and *so* want you to think I'm French

the *bleu* of the hills brings
out the crepuscular sky
a full carafe of water
or a glass of red wine?

*Joan of Arc_*Jules Bastien-Lepage_(1879)

the voices of saints compel you to approach the wilds, to look out
into an unpainted distance. skein abandoned, stool overturned,
grasping the tender leaves of a young tree. unbeknownst to you: St.
Margaret in prayer and St. Catherine in mourning. you contemplate
a barefoot path that leads into the copper-plated frame.

*Atlas*_Lee Lawrie_(1937)

between the
towers of
The Rock
I crane my
neck

interpreting
symbols
carved
into a
globe

that's
nostalgic for
progress in
the throes
of Depression

for modernity in
what a man
might become
beneath
Aquarius,
Venus,
or Mars

*Untitled (Slide)*_Carsten Holler_(2011)

a shimmering silver slide from the fourth floor to the second. how many times did we—? 8-second thrill of weightlessness. Gravity returning on a soft, black mat. getting out of the way. emerging from a flash of darkness. into the confusion of strobing lights.

*Self-portrait*_Robert Pattinson_(2020)

reflection of cool lamp light in the window. you: slumped over in a
COVID still life. the red of the room; the beige of the bowl. that might
be filled with spoonfuls of Special K. or freshly canned baked beans.
only after a bleachy wipe-down. maybe some Lysol too. but who gives
a shit? eucalyptus leaves tilt. just to meet your hopeless gaze

Acknowledgments

To my APC writing group: Nancy Agabian, Pichchenda Bao, Catherine Fletcher, Jared Harel, and Mary Lannon, thanks for helping me write even when I don't want to. To Chris Toh: you inspire me. Thanks to Tom Lombardo for seeing my work and Kevin Watson for dealing with my incessant edits. To Xinling Li, forever my first reader: it sucks that you're always right.

Vaughn M. Watson is a Pushcart Prize-nominated writer based in New York City. His poetry, fiction, and nonfiction have been published in literary journals as varied as *Tahoma Literary Review*, *About Place*, and *The Common*. *Going Out & Being Normal* was Runner-Up for the 2025 Press 53 Award for Poetry and is his debut poetry collection.

www.ingramcontent.com/pod-product-compliance
Lightning Source LLC
Chambersburg PA
CBHW021515090426
42739CB00007B/619